ABOUT THE AUTHOR

Amerah Saleh is a British Yemeni poet homed in Birmingham. She has been writing and performing for 10 years across spoken word and theatre. She has taken her poetry all around the world to share messages with young people. She is a Board Member at Birmingham Repertory Theatre, Co-founder of Verve Poetry Press and a Producer at Free Radical as part of The Beatfreeks Collective.

This is her first collection.

Twitter: @Voiceofthepoets
Instagram: voiceofthepoets
www.amerahsaleh.com

Amerah Saleh
I Am Not From Here

VERVE
POETRY PRESS
BIRMINGHAM

PUBLISHED BY VERVE POETRY PRESS
Birmingham, West Midlands, UK
www.vervepoetrypress.com
mail@vervepoetrypress.com

FIRST PUBLISHED APR 2018

Printed and bound in the UK
by TJ International, Padstow

ISBN: 978-1-912565-01-6

Dedications:

- *For my mother*
  Everything is for you, always.

- *For Yemen*
  My heart is forever yours.

- *For you*
  It has been a long time coming.

CONTENTS

I Am Not From Here

1993

"I could never hold a child in my hand one day and regret his existence the next."

You are born by accident.
You never shy away from saying this because
Yemeni's don't know how to translate "Planned
Parenthood" into Arabic.

You are named princess.
Mum told dad it was all his fault, in the delivery room
of Sorrento Hospital.
Near a roundabout on the Bristol Road is where
home found you.
Birmingham, UK.

1996

"She aligns the overused curtains across the balcony
to dry. The long grandfather clock dangles its
existence into the room to remind her of time."

In hindsight, it was only 8 hours on a direct plane to
where my mother had reminisced about for as long
as I could remember.
To me,
It was more like 8 days,
On a cramped plane heading to Yemen.
I may have been too young to understand what
people meant by home but I sure did know that this
language wasn't the one the postman spoke to me in.
I was introduced to mosquitos, grandparents,
lots of uncles and aunts.
To Bifq, cold watermelon and banana farms.
To an actual mosque that was made for actual prayer
and not for tourists.
To beaches,
seas so clear you could see the reflection of the Elephant
Mountain in them.
I was introduced to my mother's smile for the first time.

2002

"8 hours in the sky counting how many Gods I'd need to
fix us."

We had Happy Meals™ the night before.
We had met when you first came here,
tied at the hip.
Despite the Happy Meals, you cried a lot.
Not because I was leaving.
Because your ink stamp from the happy meal didn't work
and mine did.
I didn't care.
On the morning of us leaving,
you stood outside my dad's shop.
We were naïve in our byes but the tears of grief on our
cheeks matured us.
I handed you my ink toy, told you not to forget me friend.
The 8 hours this time only felt like a couple of days.
I guess that's what growing up feels like.
Things that felt so long get smaller and shorter
as life does.
Mum's smile was back.
It rained the first day we got there.
Mum said it never rains.

2004

"I have been wandering through a graveyard of your promises."

English was now secondary to our identity.
I knew how to think in English and respond in Arabic.
I learnt Adeni tea was far better than 'The English Breakfast.'
I learnt that my family in Yemen couldn't separate the British in me from the Queen.
I learnt that Sook sellers hadn't forgotten what was stolen from them.
I learnt that Yemenis are proud, that Mochas originated there even though no one drinks it.
I learnt about my mother being adopted, the history of my family.
My grandparents running a market stall selling mattresses to feed 13 children in a two bedroom flat.
My mum used to say they'd stay up late at night watching the stars top the mountains.
And that her and her siblings, 'real' or adopted, only ever spoke to each other like their blood was the same.
I learnt here, that although a daddy's girl
I would become a woman of my mother.

2007

"My stage is a bilingual picnic on a platter. A culture shock of Aseed and Full English. All my tongues sit together proudly."

I am questioning what language I think in.
If that is the reason I don't understand exams.
My bilingual processes have become burdens.
They call me Arab.
My family call me English.
I just want to be called home,
to someone,
somewhere.
My journey starts here.

2009

"Remember no matter how big and hard a mountain looks, it always crumbles down."

I   am   British.

My school tie, of Yemeni flag colours, made me feel connected.
I am self-taught in thinking and speaking in the same language.
I take stories of Yemeni women and project them on my face.
Their stories came out in my handwriting.

I felt them but I wasn't one of them.

2011

"I have 25 years of dirty water living inside of me"

In some broken homes
depression is easier to disregard than to
acknowledge.
A flight to somewhere familiar, with family,
a wedding and heat could cool situations down.
I questioned what unconditional love actually meant.
Now it is a culture of

"Pray
Drink water
Eat dates —
Depression is God calling
to Pray harder."

I was refused acknowledgement but given love.

"Go see a Sheikh."

I never wanted to not pray so much.

2014

"Until I find you, I will find solace in strangers."

This is my comfort.
I know these Brummie streets like I know a pen.
Here I know what guidance looks like.
I can write stories of women who are not here but I
give them space to live within me.
I drink coffee from Yemen to feel connected.
I put the flag next to my twitter name,
for me,
for other people to identify me.
I don't know.

2016

"I guess The American Embassy realised the 'h' at the end of my name isn't actually silent. It's Arabic."

I am a broken culture that has taught me to be too proud
to ask for help,
too vulnerable to just get over it,
too woman like to succeed.
I am proud of the broken culture I come from,
piecing myself together from family members who left
before they found themselves.
My mother's sadness lives in a Western place I call home.
Her happiness is my getaway adventure to find
myself.
I am told I am not from here.
That my ties to a piece of land is threatening to society.

I tell them,

I am not from English land.

And
I
never
want
to
be.

2017

It is in Yemen that I find the solace of belonging.

It is in Yemen that I found my mother's smile.

It is in Yemen that I realised all homes were broken.

It is in Yemen that I taught myself it is okay to think
and speak in two different languages.

That me speaking Arabic
was never exotic

but in fact,
Me.

I am home.

Not where I am,
come from,
family are from
but
who I am with,
love.

And no matter what I lose,
I have and love me,

always and forever.

2018

I trek

two buses home on cold Birmingham streets just to
see my mother's face.

I am home.

Wherever she is

is home.

Grief // Heartbreak

Pain is not the prick of a thorn
It is the companion of an ageing fortress

Sorrow is not the friend of these tears
This,

is the numbing
and cooling

of wisdom

This is the beginning of understanding
And the silent whisper between lips

Bringing a lesson with each whip of the cane
My back has become a map of the universe

Stroke your fingers down my spine
Unlock the secrets of new constellations

Grief,
Is not the Death Valley of hope

It is the chill in the stem of the rose
growing from beneath a blanket of snow

The emergence of colour.

- *by* Raza Hussain, @wuzzamill

1st September 2005

I wish I didn't have to take out your shoebox just to
remember what you looked like.
I don't even know where your grave is.
They never told me,
just so we wouldn't feel the pain, but unfortunately
with age we do.
I wish it wasn't the last day of your life that I
remembered so clearly.
I've decided I don't want a death anniversary
because I know how it feels to remember someone
solely for a whole day once a year.
I wish I remembered you more.

12th June 2013

You will learn to make those monsters friends in the
end.
People will laugh at the relationships with the people
in your head.
But you and I know,
it's harder to turn monsters into friends than it is to
turn friends into monsters.
Be proud.
Those people in your head,
well at least they talk to you.
At least they understand.

7th April 2017

I recognise the glacial silence.
It's inherited
I look around,
see tears chasing gravity on everyone's cheeks.
Pride.

31st October 2017

I was always taught not to cry.
To shush,
to be quiet
to not cause a heavy heart with tears.
I have 25 years of dirty water living inside of me.
I now know why a human being is 65% water.

It's our tears,
being told to hide away.
It's our parents
telling us to grow up.
Our teachers telling us to
'Stop crying so they can understand us.'
Our culture saying
'Tears hurt the dead.'

I am going to cry into prayer mats until they start to
mildew
in hope I can make up for lost time.

UNTITLED

The suits stood to attention,
soldiers,
cloaks and armour lined up in my cupboard.
My bow-ties like swords hung out of dead bodies.
My mattress lay still to remind me of God.
The perfumes I excessively bought smell like my
father's hair.
 I realise these items come to life at night.
And it's what I call nightmares.

Graveyards

My body is flat,
still as a fresh body in a morgue.
My mind is stood up,
a soldier,
a tower block,
an amputated arm urging up into a fist.

Snakes under the ground
have made me God fearing.
The soil is comforting me.
My blanket is full of sin.

The sin of smoking,
the sin of hoping,
the sin of love.

I am a God fearing walking sin covered in
a culture that I can't explain.

I have been running towards God
whilst my body is flat,
still,
a morgue.

The Homeless Man Who Dreams

My eye is the camera lens.
Look how I can zoom into the dirt in my fingernails
that smells like last night.
Aaaaaaaannnnd Zoom Out.
Look at how the clouds cross each other once in their
lifetime and yet they don't say hi.

"Hi mum"

I'd rather have a dead phone line being played at my
funeral than speeches about how much people will
miss me.

Every time my back remembers the feeling of shisha
pipe slashes
I take the pipe again.
Every time I see a parent hitting a child I want to
kidnap them out of love.
Every time I hear laughter I remember building dens
with my little sister using paint stained curtains
and pillows we'd secretly taken from mum's front room.

I think about a drop of water touching my scalp,
traveling to my nose, down to my chin, waistline
and onto my toes.

I would sing songs with the twins in the bath, hugs
at night, cuddles in the morning, milk stains on my
work clothes.
An exit of love with the spin as I get to the door,
forget to kiss the wife.
She calls out my name.
Oh, how could I forget, run back, kiss, and off I go.

The kids, they wait for me in the garden when I get
home, both with water guns at either side of the wall

My suit is soaked, but this is it.
Everything I've ever wanted.

I am stood in my living room, dripping out of love
whilst my wife is laughing with a towel in hand.
See we always played like this.

Zoom in; I am under a bridge that is dripping from
last nights rain.
My eyelids barely open,
I feel around me.
I need to see my life again.
I take the needle into my skin once more.

I do think about zooming into life.
I think about zooming out of life more.

Naeema

I sat on the right-hand corner of your inflatable bed.
The air is slowly being released without me realising.

I hold your hand in a crowded room of faces I've
spent years erasing,
like rubbing out pen marks with a blue rubber.
Your hands used to have potential to be Nivea model
like.
Now they're dry,
like you've given up on the chance for people to love
you.

I lean to your cold but Queen like face and call out
Nan.
It's me.
Amerah.

Your breaths
inside my head
say you know.
I am stood in a room,
hood up.
I am 8 again and you are teaching me to hold my
balance on 6 wheel rollerblades.

I am 7 again and you're sneaking us into your room to give us mint or orange club bars without our parents finding out.
I am 6 again and you are standing outside our school gates with sweets.
I am 5 again and we are feeding the ducks every Saturday in Cannon Hill Park.
I am 24 and sat beside you with my lips to your forehead trying to say goodbye.

Home // Yemen

When the Arabic alphabet climbs into my mouth,
it solidifies into salt.
Twenty-eight letters scratch my gums;
the dialect burns holes into my tongue
and I bleed conversations.

When articulation disintegrates
into the tonsils of a British accent,
I apologise.
Shame hangs from my throat
and my metallic mouth stretches
and splits
to scream:
bilingualism hurts.

Code-switching lays cement in my chest
and hardens when I reach
for the language of my ancestors,
and I cling to my ethnic name,
let it swing around my neck
from a silver chain
in attempt to use this body
and these bones to forge a route
back to the homeland that I ought to know

but don't.

Lack of fluency is endearing
when disguised as introversion,
but the voice box wasn't made
to be mute.

When my grandmother asks
how are you
in her native tongue,
my ears collapse into my temples
and my lips combust,

so I reply in English.

-*by* Afrah Yafai, @afrahyafai

Donald Trump

There is an empty solid sharp feeling that sits in the
top of my stomach,
sometimes my throat and other times in my chest.
That feeling of absolute numbness,
helplessness,
rejection.

Like black holes.
Like black holes falling into the palm of my hand
and I'm trying so hard to put them back into the sky
one
by
one.
I want them to be stars again.

My country stands on one long thread that starts in
America,
travels to Iran
and ends in Saudi Arabia.

There is a tower that has fallen on my shoulders.
It has burnt my skin,
shot me out of a dream I was so deep into for so
long.

You do not sympathise with the pain inside me,
Of being denied the soil that my mother played in as
a child.

Or
of being denied access because my mother played as
a child.

My heart.
My heart wants to fight so badly,
run away and die fighting for it.
The activist in me says go.
The realist in me says who am I?

I am merely a stone that is thrown by 10-year-old
Palestinians at an Israel Embassy
landing just an inch away from where it's meant to
be.

I am nothing.
Nothing.
I am no one.
Not even a fly on the wall of an abandoned school.
Not even a fly near 6-month-old rubbish.
Not even a citizen of Yemen.

But still,
I am rejected.

I guess The American Embassy realised the 'h' at the
end of my name isn't actually silent...
It's Arabic.

They split me open like Moses did with the Red Sea.
They don't know inside me.
I hide parts of
Exodus
and
parts of
Surat 26 Chapter 17.

Sometimes in public spaces I speak my mother's
tongue.
Not mine,
my mothers,
To remind others I am made up of old furniture from
my mum's house in Aden
wrapped in headscarves like my Nan would as though
she was ready for war
Like
Ta3aly Amerah, Wallah at'hadeek, ki3ar.

Other times,
I catch myself in the shower trying to scrub off the
smell of bakour so I can fit in.
Or
I catch myself picking my most surface level poems in
English so they can say I am western.

In England they tell me how much I don't belong,
how my hair grows funny,
my skin not the right black or white they are used to,
a little too in between.
They tell me I'm affiliated with those kinds of people.

You know,
those kinds of people.
The ones who speak Islam ...
I drown myself in ignorance because I am too tired of
fighting to fit in when in fact
I really don't want to.

Inty mish min hina they say,
Inty Britannia,
Ya3ni ma ti3rify arabi sawa,
Kalamik mukasar
Inty engleezia
I stay silent because I do not belong, yet I want to.

My mother cannot go home.
Neither can I.
Home isn't Yemen.
Home isn't here, either.
They made sure I knew that I did not belong,
Not here,
nor there ...
and now I am in between somewhere I could consider
home.

So I'm searching for home but maybe I'll never find it
in places.
Maybe god doesn't want me to get attached to
brickwork because he knows
it'll only hurt when it no longer is there.

When the gorgeous woman-like mountains that have
stood so tall for so long just fall,

all at once.
Maybe god doesn't want me to witness it.
Maybe god loves me too much to see me in pain.

Maybe I'll start searching for home in people.
Maybe home is already here and I haven't noticed.

I'll wait to hear voices from behind a screen whisper:
Psst Amerah,
Come home.

A Sorry Kind of Note

Because I am sorry that we find the easiest way to mourn,
I want to look at things through a different kind of lens.
But the lenses we are used to seem so much
easier to believe than finding a new way to look at this.

Look at me,
and tell me you're sorry so we can go ahead and move on
from things.
This was never meant to be the plan,
that hate resides in us so comfortably we forget to love.

We have forgotten the smell of love,
the calmness in the air when people are queuing up for a
public library to open.
When everyone in the queue knows we're here for one reason
only,
for knowledge.
To learn and be taught.

I am sad.
Big words that sound pretty that I wrap up in
metaphors to hide my heartbreak can be written out.
I have no other words to tell you that my heart is heavy and
pensive,
with doubts of my own beliefs right now.
With the power of my faith I know I will be okay.
We will be okay.

But who cares about us anyway?

Fire-breathing Butterflies

Inside me there were once butterflies that flew around
every time something made my heart feel soft.
Inside me those butterflies have outgrown their habitat.
I am fighting demons in my stomach.
I have swallowed my country whole by accident.

I have generations of history keeping my spine up.
Now my spine feels weak.
I can remember the smell of the air.
Like my history was decaying on mountains.
The mountains seemed happy to home it.
And now I'm not happy to home my country inside me.
I have swallowed several more alongside my own.

It's her eyes that remind me I have a beast inside me.
It's not my home,
it's hers.
But how can I forget that my home was once inside her?

There is a corrupt system inside my mind that tells me
every decision I ever made led to right now.
I am one story in more than eight billion.
One story that could have made a difference.

Because although half my home is her,
half my home is my skin.
Her home is there and I'm struggling to stay in.

There's a dragon,
poking at my belly button,
waking up.

This is Pakistan inside of me,
Saudi inside of me,
Iran inside of me,
Yemen inside of me,
America.
America is holding onto my throat.

And I don't want to swallow.
I can't take any more responsibility for hiding.
I want to shove my hand down my throat,
like its bulimia all over again.
Throw them all up to talk,
put down the weapons
argue this out.
Talk,
scream,
shout.
No winners or losers.

I want to tell them
no one owns land.
We are all made out of grains of sand.
To never forget that this world isn't ours.

We are renting it.
We need to look after it
for the generation of tomorrow.

That people may suffer now
but the future will have to deal with
consequences of mistakes that are not theirs.
Like we
are dealing with consequences that are not ours.

I want to tell them that
they are replicating the mistakes
that were made before they were born.
That this is more than one mistake.
This is more than one mistake.

This is butterflies
sick of being beautiful.
So they clipped each other's wings,
then got angry when they couldn't fly.

Not Enough

Tell me I am too English to speak fluent Arabic,
or this tongue of mine is confused of its identity.
You tell me that this body of mine is fragile
even though I carry it whole every day.
Tell me,
tell me my fingers will forget how to write and then I
won't have anything going for me.
Tell me I am not Arab enough to be human,
not human enough to be an Arab.
Tell me.
Go on, you know better than me...
Know that I am as human as my God made me.
Not perfect,
sinner
repenter.
Tell me love is only one way,
one kind.
I break it all.
Tell me I am too English,
go to elite places,
eat in English restaurants.
Tell me I am too English to speak Arabic.
I will tell you my mother taught me to think in two
languages.
My mother taught me to speak only ever in one.

Stolen Land

I am built on money stolen from my brothers in Somalia.
Built on what was once Jewish land.
Built on business,
never people.
Tell me my country is victim.
I will tell you, no,
my country is not victim,
it's not enemy
it's not rebel.
It is innocent lives that don't know how to
understand what happened.

When Saudi's say they are Saudi,
I say, no.
You derived from Yemen.
Stole from Yemen.
Took everything we own and sold it to big dogs.
Now you build monsters and tell them you help us.
Tell me how?

Tell me why my own uncle is getting rejected at your
border,
whilst his wife's house is being bombed,
bombs found that were used once
in Iraq,
told they were too dangerous to use again,
Britain stopped making
Saudi stopped buying
Or so they told us.

Tell me why my 6-year-old cousin ran with these
telling the police he's never seen them before,
that they're new.
Tell me Britain hasn't been secretly selling them to Saudi.
Tell me why they're being thrown on civilians?

Tell me why the hell my cousin recognises bombs so well?

When your whole life shifts,
at 3.56 in the morning,
you are sat on the corner of your bed with countdown playing
in the background - you realise you have been trying to build a
political status for yourself,
for a country you never believed in,
for activism that doesn't mean anything to you here.
Don't tell me that I am not doing enough,
or I should be doing more.
Or even that the foundations of me are being built.

My foundations were made in the concrete and soil of Aden,
reborn again at nine years old when families of 50+ would
gather in a one-bed house
for the sake of unity.
My foundations were made when trying to talk to doctors
became a barrier.
Language
Wahid,
Ithneen,
Arba3een duwa akalat erm shalat,

Erm haslet gamb al ga3ada
Baffled in panic and picking out what they understand.

My foundations were made in Yemen
when I realised all homes are broken.

Birmingham 2 Aden

I often wondered what you would do if I left.
Would you take a minute of silence to mourn my absence?
More like disregard the empty part of your belly
and carry on.
You are made of so much beauty.
You hide it behind walls I am not tall enough to climb.
I want to explore your body.
Some parts of you have been forbidden to me.
You break me.
Each time you make a decision for us
I break.
I fall out of love with you.

There is a battle inside my being,
of loving
of hating
and of despising who you are becoming.
You are so still in your change.
You nonchalantly brush off what they're trying to make you.
I am angry, ashamedly,
I am trying to un-love you.

When I don't want to think of you
I often take my mind to her.
Think of her Ottoman Empire like body,
the smell of her perfume reeking on my skin.
How my heart can feel broken and whole at exactly
the same time.

She never has an empty belly or lets anyone leave
with an empty stomach.
She will greet a newcomer into her home with salt
and crack an egg to remove bad spirits.
She has loved too hard and is spending her life
apologising for it.

My tongue is stained with her.
My tears taste like her water.
She is broken now
and I am stealing the bricks from my mind to fix her.
I want to fix her with each fibre of my being.
I want her to be fixed.
I know I may never see her again.
I may never be able to witness her grow again,
the way my mother witnessed her mountains rebuild
themselves from sand.

Her image has become vague.
I Google her to remind myself what she looks like.
My god, she's beautiful.
She's so beautiful.

Womxn // Identity

During the war, we moulted our
melanin through poetry and
shed our histories like unused
artillery after the rifle fire;
made ourselves comfortable in
uniforms that were too light to be warm,
in barracks too empty to be homes,
in words as colonised as our homelands.
They tasted ripe on our tongues, and we
spat them out, shell after shell as though they
didn't belong to us in the first place.
Our headscarves strangled the words right out
of our mouths, or choked them back inside
(grenades should remain untouched, sometimes.)
Eventually, we ran out of ammunition;
unable to strip ourselves of all colour,
all woman, all history, so that the enemy could

watch as we realised that
the weight of wearing our bodies
is heavier than the jagged speech that is used to

drown us.

- *by* Ahlaam Moledina

Womxn

My stage is a bilingual picnic on a platter.
A culture shock of aseed and full English.
All my tongues sit together proudly.
I am my stage in English and Arabic,
Hatha masrahi bil engleezi wal arabi.

My hijab is heavy on your lips.
Let it not be.

My womanhood is only my body.
Let it not be.

My dress sense is intimidating.
Let it not be.

This is our time to grow new foundations that allow
us all a space.

There's going to have to be a little more embracing,
a little more doing.
We need to find comfort in the uncomfortable.
A few more awkward conversations.
A few more awkward... pauses.

This is my stage - my stadium - my palace.
My voice needs raising.
Aloo sawty.
My voice needs raising.
This is my stage - my stadium - my palace.

Let my voice be the platform to raise others.
Let my words strike hearts and minds like
strings and chords.
This stage isn't just for the music.
This stage is for the curious minded,
the awake at night thinking about their future.
For the daydreamers on public transport imagining
their time in the limelight.

For the woman who prefers solace in her bedroom
rather than out in protest.
For the introverted whisperers,
we amplify your voices.
For you,
watching out the window, hoping.

For the girls who don't like heels,
put on your boots and let your footsteps do the talking.
For the ones who draw out their imperfections, perfectly.
For those who walk with their head on the ground, raise it.
For the nimble bodied and strong willed.
For the impact driven women who leave nothing and
no-one behind.

So come on, pull up a chair.
There's a seat for you too.

A Prison Guard and a Prisoner

He tells me get back in.
I tell him I can't breathe in there.
He tells me to man up.
Like manning up isn't all I've ever been told to do.
Like my hard rock hands aren't proof that that's all
I've ever done.
Like my mother isn't man enough.
He tells me to stop being a woman.
Like woman is all I've wanted to be.

My voice needs raising.
This is my stage - my stadium - my palace.

No Man

I watch men look at women in a way I'd never want
my daughter to be looked at.
In the moment of celebration,
In full-blown beards that are meant to signify respect
to a man we all live to be like.
In long white as cloud thowbs my friend got looked
at up and down as if she had stepped outdoors naked
and hadn't realised.

I felt a lump in my throat,
A thump in my chest.
A weakness in my knees but strength in my voice to
reply back.
To speak.
She thanked me for saying something,
For making her feel safe.
For making her feel like I am as protective as a man.
I am as protective as a man.
I told her,
I am as protective as I want to be around others and
this

This.
After 30 days of men caressing walls of masjids and
kneeling down more times than they do to kiss their
mothers' feet-

They celebrate the end of it with music about bitches
and hoes and comments to girls.

She grabbed my hand and we walked through crowds
of hundreds all staring at hair makeup and eyes.
And she squeezed with each stare because she knew in
my head
I was counting for statistics for my poetry.

I could never raise men.
A woman has raised me,
A woman who understands everything I happen to be
going through.
But she found it hard to raise men,
She stopped at teenager.
She stopped at toddler.
She stopped at new born for the males.

I could never raise a man.
How can I raise a man?
I have noone to say I want my children to be like you.
I could never raise a man who feels their build being
larger than a woman is something that defines them.
I could never raise a man who speaks to a mother in a
manner I wouldn't speak to an enemy in.
I could never raise a man who makes me cry myself
to sleep thinking when did it all go wrong.
I could never raise a man who disrespects his sisters
and respects his girl.
I could never raise a man who only sees his family
as a back-up plan.

I could never raise a man.
I don't think I can.
I could never hold a child in my hand one day
and regret his existence the next.

Hatija

There is a woman somewhere in the world that is
stirring her anger into food instead of words.
There is an Arab woman somewhere who is hiding
her gold-plated words in a mans back pocket
for him to never spend.

There are women, some may come in Arab forms
and some may not,
women who are on the edge of their seats waiting to
hear you speak out for them.

And there is a woman in you who is waiting for
permission to share these stories.

I, as a woman,
am stood next to you in hope
that our collective voices with oud playing will be
louder than one.

Nagiba

She is woman.
Carried her family on her shoulders throughout the wars,
throughout time, throughout generations,
throughout her life,
"Out of choice" ...
eventually.

To make sure that they are ready.
Ready to be women.

She ties her family, her children,
with a tattered plaster that doesn't stick anymore
so she adds cello tape to it to make sure it stays on.
That they stick.
That she sticks her legacy onto them.

And in all this she is seen as only woman.
A Woman.
Smaller woman.
An easier to be raped than a man kind of woman.
A wife, a chef, a cleaner, a punching bag.
Sit-al-bait type of woman.

Umi.
She is mother.
My mother.

When pressure builds...
Remember no matter how big and hard a mountain
looks, it always crumbles down.
Maybe slowly.
Maybe not in my lifetime.
But for now,
I will stay chipping away.

Noor

She is a mythical angelic light,
that sits on her tattered weathered down maglis
wondering whether
her sons are coming home for lunch.

She's cooked.
And cleaned.
She aligns the overused curtains across the balcony
to dry.
The long grandfather clock
dangles its existence into the room
to remind her of time.

Her sons are bloodied red meat rebels
fighting the devil for blessings.
Their coal stained chipped fingernails
remind them of the elbow grease
they put into home.

They wrap her in exorbitant ribbons of gold
for solitude and protection.
She,
She is the acrylic softness on a paintbrush
breastfeeding two babies at once.

Whilst her feet flake off excess of disorientated bodies
into her eye line outside.

She does not know of sons who come home.

The Only Thing My Father Taught Me

10 green bottles would be the theme tune to our
car journeys.
To us
it was a lifetime in that car.
Multiple stops.
Never ending.
We could never see the horizon.
It started in a 7 seater,
ice cold road bends,
pretend not hurting head bumps.
You'd say

"That road sign is there so you don't get lost.
On the bottom right hand side is a number.
That's the postcode.
So you never get lost,
you ring 0121 247 8797 like I taught you
And you say Ba I'm by 'B12'."

What you never taught me was to monitor
the postcodes in my mind.
When my mind wonders
from your trust
to other men's,
and I can't find my way back to my bed
I wonder,
get lost.
I haven't been found.

The doctor throws pills at me like cricket balls.
I catch every one with my mouth open.
I want to come home.
I have been wondering through a graveyard of men I have
accidentally loved.
A graveyard
of unsaid words between us.
The gates are closed.

I have been lost for a while now Dad.

Forgive Me Father

Forgive me Father.
I have taken your word and interpreted it as my own.
Taken people from you and influenced them in what I
understand.
I have skin that is coloured in colours the eye cannot bear.

For my father was never there to tell me how to make it right.
For my father has just walked back into my life.
Forgive me Father for the father you gave me has
misunderstood what it is to be a dad
I think.
For I have fought,
I have started war inside this heart of mine, that's
ultimately yours.

Father, your eyes look tired, like you've been watching out
for us whilst we have been asleep.
Father, your mind seems lost in your own words.
Father I am trying to love like I am told.
But my eyes love what they see,
hands love what they hold,
ears love the sound of those I see and hold.
Father the words you wrote down will never grow old.
So me dating seems to be out in the open and I am
figuring out what my father would have said to me
had he been the father you asked him to be.

Father, I have skin.
Skin that is brown.
Skin around edges that curve like wo-man.
Skin that gets dry.
Skin that needs cream.
Skin that needs no man to make it warm.

Skin that is scratched and skin that is torn.
Skin that has changed from when I was born.
Skin that has been on show
and skin that is hidden
Skin that is scared of love.
Skin that has been told it's forbidden.

Forgive me Father
for I have sinned.
For I have sin in me.
For I love a skin.
For sin loves me.
Forgive me Father for I have skin that sins.
Forgive me Father for I have skin.
Forgive Father for all the sin.
The sin I will do.
The sin I have to do.
Forgive me Father for the sin of me is the skin of you.

Love // Heartbreak

the smoking area in an overloaded nightclub,
a pill,
a city
to lose fragments of myself in
craving for you to present me with your love
unconscious that I could provide it to myself
convinced my ecstasy lay within you.
my love a tablespoon of vanilla essence
mixed with a shot of brown rum
that you took for granted.
now i am gifting the universe to myself.

- *by* Adjei Dsane

Solace in Strangers

I've fallen in love with a lot of strangers recently.
Not because of loneliness but rather
I am learning to find love in strangers
because they say
practice makes perfect.

The more I find love in strangers
the more likely I'll find love in you
when you arrive.
I'll be ready equipped and strong armed bruised but with
so much excellence to drown you into my arms.

I will stain my perfume on your skin
so that even when you try and scrub me off in the shower
I'll find a way for my scent to cuddle you to sleep that
night.

Every time my body feels exhausted of loving,
I will fall to my knees
and learn to love God all over again.

When my body could no longer give love to strangers,
I hope that you have found me.

I'll learn to memorise irises,
so if I find them again in 20 years,
my eyes will notice the familiarity of your pain.

When I'm falling,
I notice spider webs deconstructing all around me,
hidden barriers I've placed between
love and myself.
When I am practicing,
I am slowly
unconsciously and boldly
learning to tear them down.
When they're torn down you will find me,
in remains of spider webs,
like I've been waiting for you since before I learnt how to walk.

I will not look for you.
Just be in the right spaces where you can find me.
Hold doors for people behind me.
Say thank you to bus drivers.
Gesture
'Go ahead'
to the person in front of me in queues.

I will learn to be kind to strangers,
to park my car on their shoulders,
listen to their troubles.
I will learn to listen.
I will hold cab doors
and make food without complaining.
Run baths for you.
Stop smoke for you.
Light fires for you.
I will listen to the fire in you.

And when my phobia gets too much
I will cool us down with bubble baths.

I will use your hand as a pillow,
eyes as my mirror, so I can also learn to love
myself.

Until I find you,
I will find solace in strangers.
Until you find me,
I will continue to look for the perfect song for us,

Even if I am struggling to write the lyrics for it.

We Stand Still

You have got so much pride it walks into a room
before you do.
I need you to say sorry before I begin to beg you.
Put your hand on my chest without my assistance.
Let this body be your farm.
My lips will never attack you.
They know when it's unwanted.
My shoulders feel heavy.
And although there is nothing but traces of mud
from our fight to love last night,
I feel like your planets rest on them.
And
I'm curious to get to know them
one by one.
So, read out the alphabet and miss out f for fun.
Let me.
Give me permission to love you.

Let Me Go

We sway 46cm away from each other.
Gravity is non-existent here,
as if Isaac Newton overslept on the day the apple was
meant to fall on his head.

My body floats at 15cm,
your hands on each side of you
like we're swimming under water.

It's me.
You hover your hand around my face,.
We have lost the sense of touch.
We can only love each other with our eyes.
It seems like you're struggling.

I stare as you watch your hand,
confused of the unknown.
I am fixed on you
in this moment, so dedicated to loving your eyes,
knowing.
August Weismann explained the evolution of age
but the eyes are forever ageless.

Your confusion alarms me.
I look down at your hand now hanging around mine.
I wish I could run away but instead I levitate away
from you,
knowing you can't hold me back.

Your Therapist Is Your Lover

I left.
You didn't stop me.
Didn't message to ask where I've got.
You just ignored me.
No letters,
no texts
no calls,
I got nothing.

We went from seeing each other twice a week to
nothing.
From your face etched on my arms to no scars of you
at all..

I sat by my letterbox every morning waiting for the
shadow of the red man hoping that something of you
would fall into my arms.

On some nights when sleep felt like the end of my life,
I'd fight to keep my eyes open.
Wish you were there to listen,
to give me some of those exercises that stretched my
mind.

I'm lying if I say I coped well without you.
You never really gave me a reason to blame myself,
to grieve.

I was forced to let go.
Had to.
And I did.
None of it was a walk in the park.
It was hard man.

I wonder if I'm still in your files,
you still remember me,
if I'm just a name on old pieces of paper hidden away
from all your new lovers.
I imagine sometimes that you clear out old memories
and accidentally open me.
I worry you feel nothing.
Like you don't even remember the pronunciation of
my name.
Don't remember what I look like.
How I'd shuffle back into myself when we had an
awkward conversation,
How only you were getting me through some weeks.

4 years I dedicated to opening my soul.
You knew the names of my demons and remembered
them like they were your siblings.
You knew the beginning of anxiety,
the end of my period,
the start of depression,
the finish of us.

I think you saw it coming.
Too much of a coward to say goodbye.

Then I left.
Decided, I was okay without you.
I was ready to build my own tracks rather than walk
on yours.
I think there are two options.
You were sick of me
and wanted me to leave.
You knew I would be okay
without you.

I don't know which one hurts when either way
you've been lost in a system,
another statistic cured.
I don't know what hurts more.

That I've only been able to write this now
Or

That you still haven't sent me a letter 8 years later.
Still I am
drowning
in
your paperwork.

I Just Want to Hear Your Voice

There are voices that make dusty charcoal hearts smile.
The kind that make my voice jitter and stumble all over itself.
A voice so familiar,
it makes me wonder if my heart has been a homesick orphan
that has finally found home.
A pill of poison I have chosen to swallow.
One I would swallow,
again and again
with each societal mundane word uttered.
I enjoy the feeling of my heart falling back into place.

There are voices that make my heart ache of a familiar pain.
One that feels so old but hurts so brand new.
Sometimes it's longing,
missing or distance.
Other times it's memories,
absence or moments we'd lost in shattered glass.
We were champagne glasses dropped whilst drunk on ideas.
Our idea of love gave us both frostbite.

There are some voices that have their own DNA.
Once spoken
they are imprinted
linger in-between my fingers
find comfort in my synovium
bounce across my bedroom like Newton's cradle.
Some voices are stains on tongues for life.

Your voice makes trees stand still,
silent in moments
to greet the sound of their master.
You make my body pause for nanoseconds
before it realises
this is embarrassing.

Mi Amor

I imagine she is finding out stories of each tattoo
you've carefully inked into your skin
before I do,
finding out your darkest memories
from years I wasn't part of.
Finding the surface level
down to the dead Virgin Mary
on your inner arm by your wrist.

That she treads her warm soft hands
across your arm and
you
find comfort in her meddling,
that she wants to know
your story tonight.

She will leave
when you have just fallen asleep,
drunk on curiosity and the idea that someone
wants to hold you.

The scent of ink
and cigarette
is spinning around the room
from early hour wondrous discoveries.

I am sure
you won't remember her name,
guaranteed
she will remember yours.
Muttered under your breath
in a sweat filled club night
with a whiskey in one hand
insecurity in another.

She remembers the way your lips move when you say
your own name.
You weren't even looking when she said hers.

Coming home to nobody
is just as lonely
as coming home to somebody holding secrets disguised
as wrinkles
at the corner of their eyes.

I switch myself off paranoia mode,

tell myself words are as much a promise as touch,
that your words are a promise to us.
I stir a teabag in my mug,
thirty irritating clicks of the spoon
hitting the mug
clockwise,
in a light pink dressing gown,
a stupid lavender scented cushion in the microwave.

Sometimes I pour whiskey on my cushion cover,
imagine you
tip
toeing home from a night out.

Cuddles awaiting,
bath running,
whiskey glass on the side of the kitchen cabinet.
I like to think
I know you,
even if only a little.

Fantasy keeps us close together.
My imagination says
someone closer is better
than someone further away.
Wanting you to be loved
is a stronger desire
than me being the one.

We can say time is non existent,
a myth in our world.
5 hours behind means
5 more hours of your feet on a dance floor
with eyes wide open,
my head on a pillow
with eyes closed.

If I am not there,
how will you remember me?
You don't remember people.
You fall for stories,
my story is you.
You don't fall in love with yourself as often as I want
you to.

My tea is cold.
I forgot to take the lavender pillow out the microwave.
Your name pops up on my screen.

"Hi mujer [quien]
paso toda las hora del dia"

My body wants to hold you,
my fingers,
5,116 miles away type

"You were missed,
how was the party?"